Nothing ruins a nice summer evening like the whine and bite of a mosquito. The little bugs try to sneak up to you and fly off after drinking your blood. What do you get? A red, itchy spot, and maybe something worse. Mosquitoes spread diseases, including malaria, which kills about one million people every year. Mosquitoes also spread diseases like dengue fever, yellow fever, West Nile virus, and the Zika virus. Some people estimate that mosquitoes are responsible for half of all human deaths in history! It's enough to make you want to put on extra bug spray and slap mosquitoes good and hard every chance you get.

But not all bugs are as dangerous to humans as the hated mosquito. In fact, out of all insects, fewer than 5 percent are harmful to people. Insects are small animals with six legs and three body sections—a HEAD, a THORAX, and an ABDOMEN. At any given time there are 10 quintillion insects alive on Earth—that's a 1 with 19 zeroes following it! It's a number that's hard to even imagine. It means that for every person alive on Earth, there are over one billion insects.

Scientists have discovered more than one million different kinds of insects, and they think there could be as many as 30 million kinds in the world! There are more insects on Earth than any other kind of animal. They are our neighbors and oftentimes our quiet helpers—some clean up after us, others help us grow food, and many bugs are food for other creatures. They have been on the planet much longer than humans have. We should treat them well because they are an important part of life on Earth.

So let's meet some insects and find out what they're like. You'll find they're some of the most interesting animals in nature. You might even discover that the dreaded mosquito does some pretty cool things, too.

# BUTTERFLIES

What's the flutter? I'm a monarch butterfly. Even though monarch is another name for a king or a queen, I'm really quite humble. I'm born a simple caterpillar. I eat leaves and slink along until enclosing myself in a hard case called a CHRYSALIS. I stay in there for about two weeks. But when I finally come back out, I have these big beautiful wings! That change is called a METAMORPHOSIS.

Every winter, we monarch butterflies leave Canada and the northern United States. We don't like the cold, so we make long trips, called MIGRATIONS, to California and Mexico. But the number of butterflies making the trip keeps going down, and scientists think it's because of chemicals called PESTICIDES that farmers use to kill other bugs. We don't do any harm to farmers' fields, and we even help plants grow by spreading pollen when we stop to eat nectar from flowers. Don't bug us, so we can continue going on our yearly vacation.

# GLOSSARY

ABDOMEN—the rear segment of an insect or arachnid's body

APHID—a very small insect that eats by sucking the juices out of plants

ARACHNID—a small animal with two body segments and eight legs

BEESWAX—a substance made by bees that is used to make their honeycombs

CAMOUFLAGE—a disguise used to hide or blend in with the surroundings

CHRYSALIS—the stage of development in which caterpillars shelter themselves in a hard outer case as they grow into butterflies

COCOON—an outer case in which caterpillars shelter themselves as they grow into moths

COMPOUND EYE—an eye made up of several individual visual units

ENVIRONMENT—the world that surrounds a living thing

EXTINCTION—when no member of a species remains alive

HABITAT—where an animal or plant naturally lives or grows

HEAD—part of the body with the eyes, mouth, and brain

LARVA—the stage of an insect's life after it hatches from its egg in which it looks like a worm

METAMORPHOSIS—a series of major changes some insects go through to develop into adults

MIGRATION—moving from one place to another at different times of the year

NECTAR—the sweet liquid made by plants and used by bees to make honey

NUTRIENT—something that plants, animals, and humans need to live and grow

PESTICIDE—a chemical used to kill insects or animals that harm plants

PHEROMONE—a chemical that animals make to attract or communicate with one another

POLLEN—a fine yellow dust that plants produce that can be carried by insects or the wind to other plants in order for them to reproduce

PREY—an animal that is hunted by another animal for food

SILK—a shiny, smooth fabric made from the thread of silkworms

SIMPLE EYE—an eye with only one lens

THORAX—the middle segment of an insect, between the head and abdomen, where the legs connect

VENOM—a poison that some animals make for defense or hunting

WETLANDS—places like swamps or marshes where there is a lot of moisture in the soil

# HOW TO BE KIND TO BUGS

**B**ugs help humans in so many ways. Through pollination, bugs help the plants grow that humans like to eat. Some bugs also protect plants by eating pests that are harmful to those plants. Some bugs even eat harmful mosquitoes. We humans can enjoy products that bugs help us make, such as silk or honey.

Likewise, bugs can also be an important source of food for animals. The cycle of life is tricky, but it's also delicate. Every life-form plays an important role in its environment.

Bugs face many human-made problems such as chemicals called PESTICIDES. These chemicals are sprayed on farmers' fields to kill bugs that eat their crops. The pesticides can end up killing other helpful bugs, like bees and butterflies, as well as harming people and other animals in the area.

It's true that some bugs spread diseases, and some bugs can ruin your picnic. But likewise people can do a lot of damage to bugs. It has been estimated that as many as 44,000 species of bugs have been driven to EXTINCTION over the last 600 years. That's a lot of bugs that are gone and a lot of environments that have been changed forever!

For our own benefit, and the benefit to all life-forms and environments, it's important to remember: don't bug the insects!

## MOSQUITO

**H**ello, it's me, the mosquito. I heard what you were saying earlier—some people think that mosquitoes should just go extinct—be wiped off Earth forever! That hurts to hear! There are 3,500 different species of mosquitoes, and only 200 species attack people.

As you've probably noticed in this book, a lot of animals rely on eating bugs. In places like the Arctic, there are tons of mosquitoes, and we are a big part of the diet for all the birds that fly there during the summer. Some fish also eat us. Without mosquitoes, they might not survive. Then all the animals that eat those fish—like bears or eagles—would also have a hard time.

The fact is, all of nature is connected. No one knows what eliminating mosquitoes would do. Yes, people should protect themselves from the diseases we spread. But we're just trying to survive. Plus, we're contributing to the lives of many creatures! So be nice to mosquitoes, and be nice to all insects!

# EARTHWORMS

Oh, hi there! I'm an earthworm. I know what you're thinking. "You're in the wrong book!" I'm not an insect like an ant, and I'm not an arachnid like a spider. But hear me out!

Earthworms are very good for plants. We eat the organic matter that lands on the ground, like leaves, or we take it underground. This helps NUTRIENTS reach other plants through their roots. As we eat, we make the soil better for plants. The holes we make in the dirt allow air and water to get in, keeping plants healthy. Rich, fertile farmland may have up to 1.7 million worms in every acre!

We earthworms are great for plants, and plants are great for people. So, while you're being nice to insects and spiders, be nice to us, too.

# SPIDERS

**W**hy, hello there! I'm a spider! I'm actually *not* an insect. Remember, all insects have six legs, but we spiders have eight. We are ARACHNIDS, as are ticks and scorpions.

I know a lot of people are afraid of us spiders, which is a pity. We don't want to hurt you. Sure, some spiders are poisonous, but we only have that poison to protect ourselves and to do our favorite other activity: eating bugs.

Some of us run around on the ground hunting for bugs, but many of us build webs. It takes us about an hour to build one, although some webs take longer. We're here to help keep the number of insects from getting too high. There's nothing worse than a buggy day, right? Well, we spiders are here to help—just don't get us confused with insects. We hate that.

# GRASSHOPPER

**W**hat's *hopp*ening? I'm a grasshopper. There are over 18,000 species of grasshoppers, and we're found on every continent except for Antarctica. Wherever we live, we try to CAMOUFLAGE ourselves, which means we try to blend into our surroundings.

As our name would lead you to believe, we are great jumpers, able to leap up to 10 inches high (25 centimeters) and about three feet (one meter) long. That's 20 times our own body length! If humans could make the same jumps, at their size, a six-foot man would be able to bound 120 feet!

We eat a lot of plants, too—half our weight every day! But we also clear out some plants that get in the way of what cows and sheep are eating. And although we are eaten by birds, lizards, snakes, and even some humans, we grasshoppers have been around for at least 200 million years. Dinosaurs used to eat us, too!

## LIGHTNING BUGS

**W**hile some people call us fireflies, our light isn't hot, and we aren't flies! We're actually another type of beetle! And whether you call us lightning bugs or fireflies, we're pleased to meet you!

For many people, summer nights would be unimaginable without us blinking and flying around. Our light comes from a chemical reaction, and we shine it in order to attract other lightning bugs. The chemicals that allow us to light up have been really useful to scientists and doctors, who use it to see whether or not patients have cancer.

Unfortunately, the numbers of fireflies are going down. People aren't sure if it's because humans are building in the swamps, marshes, and forests where we fireflies like to live, or if all of the humanmade lights are making it hard for us to meet. Either way, we might be in trouble!

## PRAYING MANTISES

**O**h, hello, I'm a praying mantis. I hunt for bugs and sometimes even for small lizards or frogs. I'm a very interesting-looking bug, and I'm also very helpful. Some people will order us mantises in the mail and let us loose in their gardens. When we're small, we hunt for those pesky aphids. As we get bigger, we move on to bigger PREY. We love eating moths, crickets, flies, and other insects.

Not only do human beings keep us mantises as pets, they also consider us to be something of an inspiration. Two different styles of martial arts from two different parts of China are based on our aggressive hunting style. Pretty cool, huh? It's a good reason not to bug praying mantises!

## BEE FACTS

- The oldest known bee fossil is 100 million years old.

- Bees have five eyes—three "**SIMPLE EYES**" and two "**COMPOUND EYES**."

- They flap their wings 240 times per second to stay in the air.

- Not all bees have stingers. Only female bees of certain species can sting, and their stingers contain a poison called **VENOM**—but don't worry. Bee stings may hurt, but unless you're allergic or get stung a lot of times, they are not dangerous.

- Only 15 percent of bees live in colonies like hives. Most bees are solitary.

- Honeybees can fly 15 miles per hour.

## BEES

What's the buzz? We're bees! You should be nice to us because we're really important, not just for people, but for the whole planet!

You probably knew that humans sometimes keep beehives to enjoy BEESWAX and honey. But bees do something else, too: we pollinate plants. Bumblebees and honeybees land on flowers to collect NECTAR and POLLEN, which we take home to the hive to feed our young. While we're on a flower, a powdery pollen gets all over us. As we fly onto the next flower, we spread that pollen. Spreading pollen helps plants create new seeds to make new plants. If there weren't any bees, humans and other animals would have trouble finding fruits and vegetables they need to eat. But bees are in danger! Many bees are dying, and people think it could be because of chemicals, called pesticides, that humans spray to keep pests away from plants. Protecting bees will help not only humans but also plants!

# CRICKETS

You might be used to hearing from us crickets. We're that lovely soundtrack you hear on a summer's night. We make noise by rubbing our wings together. You might not know that our ears are actually on our knees! Crickets also make more noise when it's warm out, so we're kind of like little thermometers! Just listen to how many cricks a single cricket makes in 15 seconds and add 37 to it. Then you'll know the temperature in degrees Fahrenheit!

Crickets are super-important to the environment. Even though it's not fun for us, we crickets are a popular snack for frogs, snakes, lizards, and birds. Even some other bugs eat us. We're also popular with humans. In some places, people keep crickets as pets, because they enjoy listening to our sounds and watching us live our cricket lives.

# WASPS

Hey, I'm a wasp. You're probably not always too glad to see me, and I understand that. We wasps have these big stingers and, gosh, do they hurt!

But while you should probably leave us alone if you come across one of our nests, you don't have to be afraid of wasps. Do you know who should be afraid of wasps? Caterpillars. We love eating those things. And the caterpillars, well, they love to eat your plants! So go easy on us wasps; we're on your side!

## DRAGONFLIES

**H**i, I'm a dragonfly, and if you hate mosquitoes, you should be nice to me! Have you ever heard the saying "the enemy of my enemy is my friend"? Basically, I love to eat mosquitoes, so you should love me! I can eat as much as a fifth of my own body weight in bugs every day.

When we're born, we dragonflies live underwater, where we eat other freshly hatched insect LARVAE that might be swimming around. The problem is, a lot of the world's WETLANDS are being drained and dried out because of humans. That makes life hard for us. It sure would be nice for us if wetlands and marshes were protected. Think of how much we could help you!

## BEETLES

**H**i, I'm a beetle! There are so many different types of beetles—almost one in every four species on Earth is a type of beetle. You've already met the dung beetle, but did you know the ladybug is also a type of beetle? We really are a helpful bunch. Some of us are even fashion models: people have been making jewelry that looks like the scarab beetle ever since the time of Ancient Egypt!

Some of us, unfortunately, are put in a position where we are bad for plants or for buildings. I'm an Asian longhorned beetle, and I can kill trees. I don't mean to harm the trees, but when people build over our homes, we end up where we aren't wanted. When our HABITATS are destroyed, we have to go somewhere. You wouldn't be mean to a guy just because he's lost, would you?

# ANTS

**H**i there; we're ants! There are more than 13,000 different kinds of ants. Some of us live underground, others of us live in trees, and many of us may be living right in your own backyard. Did you know that some ants, called honeypot ants, make honey like bees? Or that the army ants of the rain forest are poisonous?

But don't worry! Even poisonous ants are helpful to the ENVIRONMENT. You may have heard that ants can lift up to five times their own weight—it's true!—and many of us use that strength to dig! Every year the world's ants dig up more than 16 billion tons of dirt! Moving the dirt around also moves around nutrients, which helps plants grow. We also clean up decaying plant matter and eat harmful pests. Be nice to ants. We're making your life easier!

# DUNG BEETLES

Now, I know what you're thinking: dung beetles, ew!

Sure, we dung beetles have a sort of smelly life—we collect poop from animals. Sometimes we roll it into a ball and bury it, which is good for the soil. Other times we drink the juices straight from it. I get it: That type of life isn't for everybody. In fact, it would make most animals sick.

But I'm happy to do it! And you should be glad that I am. Otherwise all that smelly waste would just pile up! Life without dung beetles would stink! So, leave us alone, would ya?

# LADYBUGS

**W**hy, hello there, stranger. I'm a ladybug! You might recognize me from my red shell with black spots. Did you know that some of us have no spots at all, or that some of us are orange? But we ladybugs aren't just stylish and good-looking. We're helpful to have around the garden, too.

See, one of the worst pests for a garden are these little green bugs called APHIDS. They eat plants, like rosebushes, until the plant dies. But we ladybugs love to eat aphids! Over a lifetime, a ladybug will eat up to 5,000 aphids. It's no wonder that some people say ladybugs are good luck! Don't bug ladybugs, and we'll protect your flowers!

# SILKWORMS

**O**h, hello there, I'm a silkworm. Don't let my name fool you, though, I'm not really a worm. I'm actually a caterpillar. In order to grow up, I make a COCOON around myself. Then, just as some caterpillars turn into butterflies, I morph into a moth.

But people have been disturbing my sleep for over 5,000 years! The cocoon I make is made with a single fiber. This allows people to weave cocoons together into a soft, beautiful fabric called SILK. The traditional way of making silk involves boiling the cocoon, which kills the caterpillar in the process. There are new methods to produce a fabric called Ahimsa silk, or peace silk, that is safe for the caterpillars. The caterpillars climb out of their cocoons first and then the cocoon is harvested. The silk looks slightly different than the kind produced in traditional ways, but it's still beautiful. And there's a certain beauty to being nice to us silkworms, too.

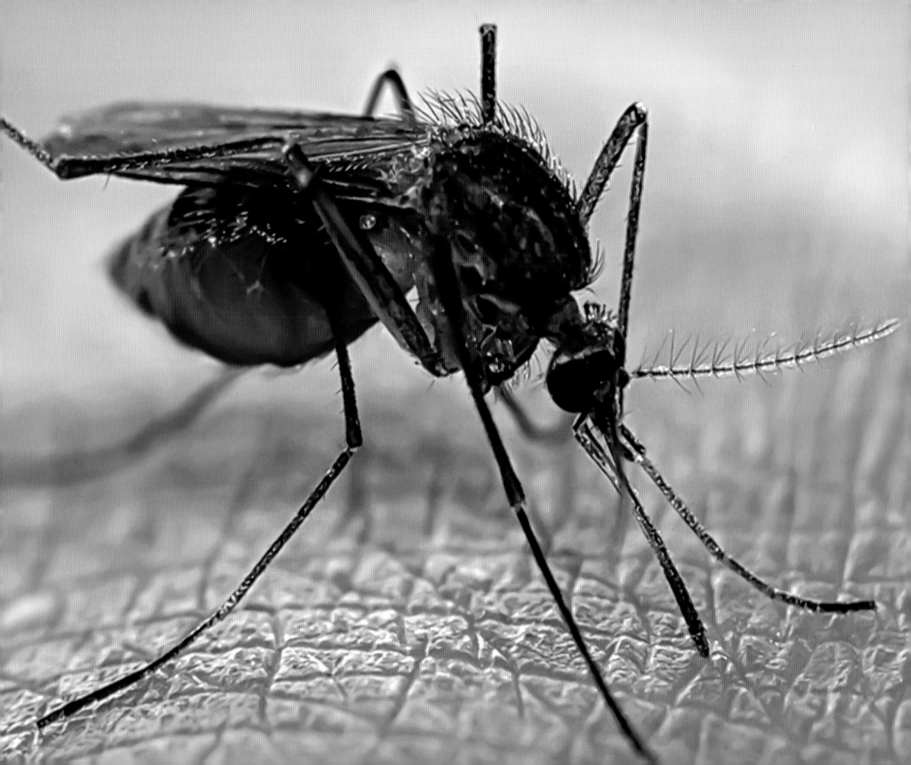

# DON'T BUG
## the INSECTS

### Fascinating Facts about Nature's
### Most Misunderstood Creatures

by Ben Richmond

STERLING CHILDREN'S BOOKS
New York

**STERLING CHILDREN'S BOOKS**
New York

An Imprint of Sterling Publishing Co., Inc.
1166 Avenue of the Americas
New York, NY 10036

Text © 2017 by Ben Richmond
Alamy:  © Jeff Lepore: 14
iStock:  © assalve: 19; © avid_creative: back cover; © Boogich: 12; © dennisvdw: 30;
© Fatman73: 10; © HAYKIRDI: 6;
© IMNATURE: 8; © imv: 16; © jimcloughlin: 24; © KirsanovV: 22; © Pobytov: 15; © Savushkin: 3;
© StockPhotoAstur: 20
Minden Pictures:  © Kim Taylor/NPL: 5
Shutterstock:  © Brandon Alms: 21; © encikAn: 17; © jdm.foto: 23; © khlungcenter: 25;
© Lori Labreque: cover; © Paul Looyen: 29; © john michael evan potter: 11; © Daniel Prudek: 18;
© Tischenko Irina: 27; © Wasan Ritthawon: 13; © Sofiaworld: 9

ISBN 978-1-4549-2137-0

Library of Congress Cataloging-in-Publication Data

Names: RIchmond, Benjamin, 1986- author.
Title: Don't bug the insects / Ben Richmond.
Other titles: Do not bug the insects;
Description: New York, NY : Sterling Children's Books, an imprint of Sterling
    Publishing Co., [2017] | Audience: Ages 6-10
Identifiers: LCCN 2016048473 | ISBN 9781454921370
Subjects: LCSH: Insects—Juvenile literature.
Classification: LCC QL467 .2 .R538 2017 | DDC 595.7—dc23 LC record available at
https://lccn.loc.gov/2016048473

Distributed in Canada by Sterling Publishing Co., Inc.
c/o Canadian Manda Group, 664 Annette Street
Toronto, Ontario, Canada M6S 2C8
Distributed in the United Kingdom by GMC Distribution Services
Castle Place, 166 High Street, Lewes, East Sussex, England BN7 1XU
Distributed in Australia by NewSouth Books
45 Beach Street, Coogee, NSW 2034, Australia

For information about custom editions, special sales, and premium and corporate purchases, please contact Sterling Special Sales at 800-805-5489 or specialsales@sterlingpublishing.com.

Manufactured in China

Lot #:
2  4  6  8  10  9  7  5  3  1
03/17

www.sterlingpublishing.com